FISHING AUSTRALIA

Trout & Freshwater

POCKET GUIDES

COMPILED BY
LAWRIE McENALLY
& JULIE McENALLY

CONSULTANT EDITOR
STUART McLAUGHLIN

Jim: ... a little something to help you plan your fishing trip to Oz!! Happy reading. Love Val & Nev

BayBooks
An imprint of HarperCollins*Publishers*

STOCKISTS:
Mosman Antique Centre
700 Military Road
Mosman NSW 2088
Ph: (02) 968 1319

Tully's Northside Timber Stripping and Finishing
Ph: 018 609 793

A Bay Books Publication

Bay Books, an imprint of
HarperCollins*Publishers*
25 Ryde Road, Pymble, Sydney, NSW 2073, Australia
31 View Road, Glenfield, Auckland 10, New Zealand

First published in Australia in 1994

National Library of Australia
Cataloguing-in-Publication Data:

McEnally, Lawrie.
Trout and freshwater.
Includes index.
ISBN 1 86378 184 6.
1. Fishing – Australia. 2. Freshwater fishes – Australia. 3. Trout fishing – Australia. I. McEnally, J.M. (Julie Maree). II. Title. (Series: Fishing Australia pocket guides).
799.110994

The publishers gratefully acknowledge the assistance of the many contributors to Fishing Australia.

COVER:
Photography by André Martin
Styling by Louise Owens
Timber cylindrical container and hand reel from Mosman Antique Centre
Block (for block and tackle) from Tully's Northside Timber Stripping and Finishing

Printed in Australia by Griffin Press, Adelaide

9 8 7 6 5 4 3 2 1
97 96 95 94

CONTENTS

INTRODUCTION

Trout and temperate freshwater fishing are among the most popular forms of angling in the country.

Trout are found in the cool high country, often in places of great beauty. This magnificent, natural backdrop makes trout fishing an exceptionally rewarding experience.

Trout are often stocked in waterways, keeping their numbers high and providing good catch rates for anglers. They are a top fish both to catch and to eat.

Freshwater fishing in the bush is also great fun, particularly fishing for Australia's own native fish. You can do this in the inland or on the freshwater stretches of our coastal streams.

Amongst the temperate freshwater fish is the mighty Murray cod or Goodoo as the Aborigines called it. This is one of the great freshwater fish of the world and a worthy opponent.

Adding spice to the temperate freshwater scene are the introduced species like carp and redfin. While they have caused their share of problems they are here to stay and are available for anglers to catch.

This book sets out the best ways to catch both trout and temperate freshwater fish. It provides all the information needed by anglers learning about these fish as well as more in-depth material for experienced anglers.

Few forms of fishing are more absorbing, more relaxing or more attractive than angling for trout and other freshwater fish.

Rainbow trout.

TROUT AND SALMON

Trout and salmon are not native to Australia: they are introduced fish that have been acclimatised.

Known generally as salmonoids, this group of fish has had an interesting and colourful career in Australian fishing.

Brown trout were the original introduced species from Europe back in the last century. The introduction of American rainbow trout followed a few decades later.

These fish along with redfin, carp and a host of other animals and birds were introduced by the colonists to provide them with sport and game of the type they had had at home in Mother England.

Most of the introduced species went on to become feral pests but the trout, limited to cold climate areas by water temperature tolerances below 20°C, became an accepted part of the Australian fishing scene.

There are actually five major salmonoid fish available to anglers.

Brown Trout

Brown trout have adapted well to Australian conditions and have a higher water temperature tolerance than rainbows.

Browns tend to be keen bottom feeders, particularly in the big lakes, favouring yabbies, shrimps and mudeyes.

In the rivers they tend to be wily, cautious opponents often magnificently marked with big, black speckles.

Rainbow Trout

The rainbow trout prefers cool water but is an extremely active, inquisitive feeder.

The rainbow is generally regarded as easier to catch than the brown, but this depends as much on where and how you fish as anything else.

In the lakes, the rainbows spend a lot of time in mid-water and near the surface, often feeding heavily on tiny water fleas.

The rainbow is a great acrobat when hooked and the fish is a top fighter on light tackle.

Brook Trout

The brook trout is actually a char, but whatever its family history this fish has not been a successful introduction.

Tens of thousands of brook trout fingerlings have been dropped into rivers and dams in good trout country but the returns have been minuscule.

Brown trout.

Brook trout.

Only an odd brook trout turns up in anglers' catches, although a few are caught each year.

These distinctly shaped and marked fish cannot be confused with any other trout when captured.

Atlantic Salmon

Atlantic salmon have become a huge industry in Tasmania where enough farm stock have escaped to provide quite reasonable fishing in places like the Huon estuary and other river systems.

Atlantic salmon are also reasonably common in Lake Jindabyne in the Snowy Mountains as a result of stocking by NSW Fisheries.

Otherwise their history is very much like that of the brook trout, extensively stocked but rarely ever caught.

When hooked, these fish display more power than either rainbow or brown trout, particularly when striking a lure.

These fish are easily mistaken for rainbow trout but can be distinguished by their deeply forked tail compared to the even curve of the rainbow trout's tail.

Quinnat Salmon

The quinnat salmon has been established in Victoria's Lake Purrumbete as well as a few other Victorian lakes.

These great fighters grow fast and are a superb fish to capture.

The only problem is that they seem to have very particular demands about where they live with only Lake Purrumbete being genuinely successful so far.

Whichever species you catch, there is something quite special about fishing for trout and salmon. They live in some of the most spectacular and scenic areas in the country. They fight in acrobatic fashion, respond to a wide variety of angling techniques and are very good eating. Trout and salmon are complete sport fish and great fun to catch.

Head of an Atlantic salmon with hooked jaw.

TROLLING FOR TROUT

Trolling is a reliable and fun way to catch trout. It is particularly popular on the highland lakes and impoundments but it can also be used on some of the larger rivers in trout territory.

Like many things in fishing, trout trolling can be as simple or complex as the angler cares to make it.

In its simplest form it is no more than tying on a lure and dragging it behind a moving boat. In its more complex form it involves fish attractors, echo sounders, downriggers, rod holders and a wide variety of lures.

For the novice angler it can be the best way to catch that first trout, simply because the boat makes a lot of territory available.

To be successful at trolling, a few basic principles need to be followed and these can be added to as the angler's experience builds.

The Boat

The boat plays two vital roles in trout trolling. It is the vehicle used to present the lure and it is the fishing platform for the anglers.

The most important requirement of the boat is a capacity to operate at very slow speeds for long periods of time.

The trolling speed for trout is mostly 1 to 2 knots, so trolling with large outboards is not really feasible. If the main engine is over 15 hp then a smaller engine will be needed for trouble-free trolling.

Fit Out

To help make trolling more comfortable and more productive, the boat can be fitted with rod holders and a range of modern technology.

Rod holders have two important functions: they save the angler the tiresome job of holding the rod, and they keep the rod in the desired set position. Rods supported in a rod holder also set the hook better than rods that are hand-held.

Comfortable seats and cushions also make long hours of trolling more comfortable. An extension tiller for the outboard is handy so the vessel can be controlled from the most comfortable steering position.

Technology plays an important part in trout trolling. Most keen trollers use an echo sounder or fish finder of the LCD or video type. The sounder has a range of roles. It can and will locate fish. It shows the depth at which the fish are swimming and it will show columns of water fleas which rainbow trout find particularly attractive.

Finally, it also shows the bottom,

submerged trees and other underwater structures. This allows the skipper to keep the lures from being snagged or to follow depth contours that are producing fish.

Hire Boats

For anglers visiting a trout area it is likely that hire boats will be available. These are mostly well engined for trolling but will only have rod holders at best. Most hire boats are fairly spartan but they do provide access and good results can still be achieved. The one thing you should always put in a hire boat is a pillow: metal seats in trout country get cold and hard.

Tackle

The best tackle for trolling is a small to medium-sized baitcaster reel on a lightweight rod with a 30 to 40 cm long butt. The reel should be loaded with 6 kg line.

Baitcasters avoid line twist problems which can occur when using fish attractors like cowbells on threadline-type reels.

Threadline- or spinning-type reels are most useful when trolling lures without the addition of fish attractors. The rod and reel should be lightweight and line of 3 to 4 kg is standard.

Lures

The range of lures that will actually catch trout is huge. The walls of tackle shops attest to this. For anglers new to trout fishing, knowing just what to buy can be difficult.

As a guide, the following set of lures would perform well when trolled in most trout waters.

Helin Flatfish, size X4, colours: frog (FR), pink (PI) and gold (G).

Kwickfish, size K8, colours: frog, brown trout.

Tassie Devil/Cobra types, size 50 mm, colours: gold, perch scale, pink and black.

Celta, size No. 2, colours: red or red/black/gold. Other similar bladed spinners are also useful.

Catch of quality lake trout.

Wet flies, Matuka, size medium, colours: black, black and red, green.

There are plenty of other lures worth using and if you want to give a few extra models a try, ask at the tackle store in the area being fished what is working and they will usually provide good advice.

Fish Attractors

Fish attractors of various types can improve catch rates on trout, particularly in the highland impoundments. Fish attractors are either a set of spinning blades on a wire, and known by various brand names such as Cowbell, Ford Fender or Bolo, or a highly polished piece of sheet metal known as a Dodger.

The flash and noise generated by these attractors draw the trout from either curiosity or territorial aggression and it then grabs the lure attached half a metre or so behind the attractor.

The lure is joined to the attractor by 30 to 40 cm of 3 to 4 kg line. The idea behind this is that should the rig snag, the lure will break off before the more expensive attractor. That is why the baitcasters are loaded with 6 kg line.

Technique

The aim of trolling is to cover as much water as possible and to present the lures to as many fish as possible.

This usually means working around a lake following the contours of the shoreline, submerged tree line, or the underwater geography.

The lures are set 20 to 50 m behind the boat. Usually four rods are the maximum that can be set and controlled from a small boat. Two should be close to the boat (approximately 20 m and two should be well out (approximately 40 to 50 m).

The height of the rod tip off the water will also affect the depth at which lures run: the closer the rod tip is to the water, the deeper the lure will run. So low-slung or height-adjustable rod holders are best. They also enable maximum separation space for the lures being trolled.

The lures can be set with or without fish attractors: it depends on personal choice. The fish attractors tend to spoil the fight of the fish but generally catch more fish, so it depends on whether you want fish or sport.

The fish attractors take the lures down

Brown trout taken trolling with Cowbells.

much deeper than a lure on its own, so you can cover different water levels by fishing some lures with attractors and some without. There are also times when the fish want to take lures only with or only without the attractors, so you need to offer them some choice.

The reels are set with a light to medium drag so the striking fish can take line but with enough tension to set the hooks and control the fish during the fight.

When a fish strikes the motor is thrown out of gear, the angler takes the rod and the other passengers wind in their rods.

Once the fish is netted the boat goes back into gear and the anglers reset the lures.

If you take a fish, go back and work the spot again as several trout will often hold in a particular area, although they don't school in the same manner as saltwater fish.

On any given day the fish may show a decided interest in one colour or one lure pattern. For example, if only lures with gold colour are being taken, then changing all the lures to patterns with gold in them should yield more strikes. The same applies if only one lure pattern is being taken consistently: add another lure just the same to increase the strike rate.

If using an echo sounder always note the depth where the strikes occur. Often the fish are at one depth and following that depth contour can result in more strikes.

The sounder will also tell you if the water is getting too shallow and you need to move out wider to avoid snags. You will learn quickly that your lures, particularly the attractors, have an operating depth. When the water shallows to that depth they will snag. The lures can be raised to clear an obstruction by increasing boat speed.

Boat Speed

Boat speed can be a vital factor in getting strikes when trolling. Lures like Flatfish and Kwickfish work best at very slow speeds, while lures like Tassie Devils and Cobras need more speed to work well. Watch the lures carefully beside the boat before you pay them out to ensure that the speed used has them swimming seductively.

It is advisable to alter speeds a little every fifteen minutes or so to establish the fish's preference. Don't spend the whole day trolling at just the one speed; mix the revs up a bit until you establish what speed is attracting the strikes.

Tackle Back

One essential item in every lake troller's tackle box is a Tackle Back. These simple lure retrievers are clipped onto the angler's line when the boat is directly above the snagged lure.

The Tackle Back then slides down the taut line and drops over the attaching snap swivel.

The light cord holding the Tackle Back is then lifted and the lure or attractor is pulled free of the snags. Tackle Backs save heaps of gear.

FINDING LAKE TROUT

Finding lake trout can be daunting to those new to trout fishing due to the large expanses of water and seemingly featureless shorelines.

Within the lake system, the trout actually use every available food source. Sometimes almost all the trout will be doing the same thing but usually they are spread out with some in each feeding area.

Each lake will have its own characteristics but there are some general rules that hold true almost everywhere.

The trout will be feeding or moving relative to their physical demands or available circumstances. They seek food, shelter, acceptable water temperatures and they move up streams to breed.

Rising Water

When lakes are filling rapidly after rain or with snow melt, the rising water will be covering new ground and forcing worms, insects, grubs and other bits and pieces out of the ground.

At this time large numbers of trout will be found feeding close to the shoreline. They will feed in the near shore areas at night and in the early morning or late afternoon, falling back into the deeper water as the sun gets fully up.

When the water is rising, baits of worms and mudeyes work best. In periods of falling water the trout will tend to use the shallow bays rather than graze around the shoreline.

The treed edges of a lake are always a likely spot.

Shallow Bays

Shallow bays, particularly those with a good growth of aquatic weeds, are used as grazing areas by the trout. Here they find lots of aquatic insects, snails, yabbies, shrimps and small fish.

Being shallow these areas also fish best at night or in periods of low light.

Deep Shores

Deep shorelines will produce fish during the middle of the day as they allow the angler access to deeper water where the trout will feed without feeling threatened.

The ends of spits or fingers of land that jut out into the lake can also be similarly productive.

Trees

Many lakes have huge areas of drowned timber from when they were filled. These drowned forests provide a great habitat for both mudeyes and yabbies.

The trout know this and regularly use these areas as hunting grounds.

The treed bays and shorelines can be hard to fish as they are basically full of snags. Best results will come using bubble floats and baits suspended off the bottom.

Timbered shorelines are very reliable locations in most dams.

Rivers and Creeks

Any stream that flows into the dam will be regarded as a potential food source by the trout. There will also be some exchange of fish coming into the lake or entering the river.

The stream carries lots of food and trout will regularly feed where even quite small creeks enter a lake. These areas are always worth prospecting.

Breeding Season

Brown and rainbow trout have distinct breeding seasons. They gather in big numbers in the areas leading up to their breeding grounds in the weeks prior to spawning.

Steeply sloping banks are good spots for spinning and fly fishing.

In mainland Australia, the browns gather in late May or early June and the rainbows in late September and early October.

Some of these runs of spawning trout are quite famous, for example at Providence Portal at the entrance to the Eucumbene River and at Waste Point on the Thredbo River on Lake Jindabyne.

These pre-spawning trout are often very aggressive and easily caught, particularly on lures.

Water Temperature

Water temperature can be a critical factor in locating lake trout.

In the hot summer months the surface temperatures often become too warm and lacking in oxygen for the trout. At these times they retreat to deeper, cooler waters returning to feed in the shallows at night or early in the morning.

In warmer months always look to deeper water for best catches.

BUBBLE FLOATS FOR TROUT

The technique of bubble floating for trout is immensely popular and extremely effective.

Bubble floats are plastic or soft rubber devices. Most are spherical or egg-shaped. Their most distinctive design feature is their ability to be partially filled with water to provide casting weight for the presentation of ultralight baits.

The soft plastic or rubber bubbles traditionally feature little slits through which they can be filled. The float is simply squeezed to expel air, then held underwater and allowed to suck water in through the slit.

Hard plastic bubbles have one or more holes fitted with little plugs or bungs which can be removed for filling the float.

All bubble floats have some form of line attachment device. Most of the soft rubber varieties have little 'ears' with holes for the line, while the hard plastic versions mostly have a central line channel like that of a bobby cork.

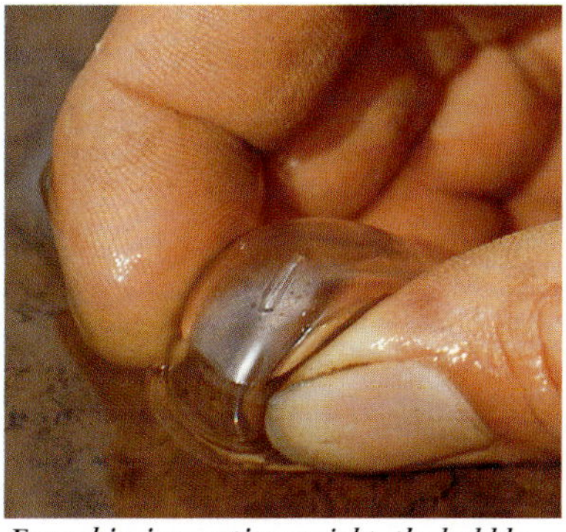

For achieving casting weight, the bubble float is filled with water.

Although they can be used for all kinds of fishing in both salt and fresh water, it is in the field of bait fishing for trout — especially in lakes and dams — that bubbles really shine.

THE BUBBLE CONCEPT

The idea of the bubble is to combine a casting weight and a float in one device.

By adding water to the bubble, one can achieve the casting weight necessary to throw a worm, minnow, mudeye or grasshopper a considerable distance without the need for sinker and shot.

Then, when the bait splashes down, you have a float which will support the bait at a predetermined depth.

BUBBLE FLOAT DRAWBACKS

The negative aspects of bubble floats are their relative bulk, the fairly big splash they make when they hit the water, and the drag or resistance they present to a softly biting fish. Happily, this last problem can be largely avoided through some of the rigging techniques we will discuss further on.

However, bubble floats cast much further than quill-type floats and lack the 'anchoring' hassles and snag-up problems of sinker-type bottom rigs.

Bubble float rigs also account for a great many quality trout each year.

Baits for Bubbling

The most common baits employed by bubble floaters are mudeyes, minnows and gudgeons, earthworms and scrub worms, witchetty grubs, grasshoppers, crickets and maggots.

For the most part, however, it is mudeyes and minnows that are most often selected as baits.

Tackle for Bubble Floating

Bubble floats can be used off all sorts of gear. However, the ideal bubble floating outfit consists of a small to medium threadline reel filled with 2 to 4 kg line and combined with a light, relatively slow taper rod of 2 to 2.5 m length.

This longer-than-standard rod allows easier casting of deep rigs and more line control with a drifting float. It is also advantageous in quickly picking up slack for a strike.

The use of a trace or leader on most rigs is also recommended. Generally, 3 kg main line and 1 to 2.5 kg leaders are suggested, though in tough country or big fish territory, 4 kg main line and 3 to 3.5 kg traces may be advisable — even essential.

A few soft split shot, some tiny No. 14 brass swivels and a range of short-shank hooks in sizes No. 12 to 6 round out the necessities.

Rigging your Bubble

The most basic bubble rig sees the float firmly fixed on the main line anywhere from half a metre to 3 m or more above the baited hook.

This rig is rather clumsy and presents maximum resistance to the biting trout, which must either pull the float under or drag it across the water, but it does catch fish.

The other disadvantage of this fixed rig is its unwieldiness when casting, especially if using dropper lengths greater than 1.5 or 2 m.

Big catches of trout can sometimes be made using bubble float techniques.

An improvement is the running bubble. Here, a partially filled bubble is run on the main line below a stopper such as a tiny swivel, piece of wool or sliding rubber stop.

This rig is easier to cast, but still presents drag problems with soft-biting trout.

One rig that avoids this problem does away with the idea of depth setting by completely removing the stopper.

In this rig, the bubble runs freely on the main line above the bait — usually above a swivel or float stop that prevents the bubble running right onto the hook.

Because there is no stopper, the bait is free to slide slowly towards the stream or lake bed. In calm, still water, that's exactly where it will end up in time — which may be a plus or a minus, depending on where you are fishing.

By greasing the line with a line dressing or vaseline, you can slow up or even stop the sink rate.

Open Bail and Greased Line

Whichever rigging technique is chosen, most bubble float anglers working the calm waters of lakes and dams prefer to fish with their reel's bail arm open.

This way, when a trout picks up the bait and moves off, line is free to trickle from the spool, creating the minimum drag and resistance. Baitrunner reels also work very well using this system.

The entire process is greatly facilitated and enhanced if the line between the rod tip and the float is greased so that it will float on the surface of the water.

Heavily timbered areas are ideal for bubble floating.

Failure to grease the line will cause it to sink and form a deep belly between the angler and the float. This creates drag which may deter a biting fish. The belly may also foul in sunken trees or weed beds.

Purpose-made line floatants such as Mucelin are best for the job, though vaseline works just fine. Simply apply a little to the fingertips or a scrap of rag and wind the line through this to apply a coating. You need only grease the 'working' length of line: about 30 m or so.

All dressings and greases wash off in time. Reapply the grease at the start of each fishing session, and do it again after three or four hours of use.

Try the Bubble

Bubble floats are a valuable addition to the tackle boxes of all freshwater anglers, especially those targeting trout in still water, so try the bubble when next you bait fish.

BAITS FOR TROUT

Trout will eat a very wide variety of food, but like most species they have preferences. Sometimes these preferences can drive an angler to distraction but as a rule good baits get eaten.

Trout are active hunters and prefer their food live or lifelike. In most trout areas, basic baits like worms and mudeyes can be purchased but other baits like shrimps and yabbies need to be captured.

Bait presentation is an essential part of the system. It is important to present the bait naturally, alive and in a manner that makes it vulnerable to attack from trout.

Worms

Worms are the great freshwater stand-by. They can be purchased or dug and there are several different varieties that are available. Worms are fairly tough and last well on a hook. They also keep and carry well.

Most common are red wrigglers which are farmed, and garden and scrub worms, which need to be dug or purchased.

Large active scrub worms are a great bait for trout.

When presenting worms, small, light hooks are best as they allow the worm to wriggle seductively, without killing the bait.

Worms are easily farmed at home and you can even buy commercial worm boxes so you have plenty of fresh, wriggling worms whenever you go fishing. The worms are fed on domestic vegetable scraps.

Mudeyes

Mudeyes are the larvae of dragonflies and are keenly hunted by trout. Despite being small and fragile, they are exceptional bait.

Mudeyes are found under and in drowned timber in lakes, pools and farm dams. It is easy to collect them if you have the time or they can be purchased.

The best presentation for mudeyes is to use a very fine No. 10 size hook and conceal the hook within the abdomen of the mudeye. The bait is then fished on a very light 2 kg trace and suspended under a bubble float.

Buying mudeyes can seem expensive but they do get eaten.

The secret with mudeyes is to take the time to learn how to present and cast them properly (*see* **Mudeyes**, p. 19).

Yabbies

Yabbies are a major dietary item of lake trout, particularly bottom-dwelling browns. The large brown trout can catch and consume yabbies up to 10 cm or more in length, although smaller yabbies around 5 cm seem to work better as bait.

Anglers can catch yabbies in traps baited with meat or fish heads or with a scoop net and torch at night around the foreshores of the lake.

The best way to hook a yabby is once only through the tail with a No. 4 to No. 1 size hook. Just remember to use a rig that suspends the bait off the bottom. If set on the bottom the yabby will drag itself under the nearest rock or tree and snag you.

Shrimps

A sometimes underrated trout bait, shrimps are extremely successful when fished under bubble floats in the same manner as mudeyes.

Shrimps inhabit almost all lakes and streams and trout accept them readily. Shrimps can be captured in baited traps, which are as simple as a tin with holes punched in it, or in commercial fine mesh traps.

Freshwater shrimp are an underrated and effective trout bait.

Best catches of shrimps will come from around areas with plenty of aquatic weeds, fallen timber or heavily grassed banks partially submerged in water.

Grasshoppers

When grasshoppers are flying in midsummer many of them end up trapped on the surface of both lakes and rivers. At this time, trout hunt them avidly.

Grasshoppers carefully presented on a small hook are a top trout bait in summer.

Grasshoppers are easily captured using a fine net while walking in long grass.

They are baited by using a small No. 8 hook placed through the base of their wings. The wings are quite tough and will hold a hook firmly.

The hopper is usually fished either unweighted on a stream or unweighted but using a bubble float for casting weight on the dams.

Wood Grubs

Although usually associated with native freshwater fish like Murray cod and yellowbelly, small wood grubs and similar beetle larvae are also attractive to trout, particularly if fishing at night or in dirty water.

Frogs

Although legal in some states the authors do not recommend the use of frogs. They are an amphibian and an important part of the wetlands ecology and are not needed as bait.

Bait Fish

Trout will take bait fish readily but transporting all sorts of live fish around on trout streams and lakes is generally frowned upon, mostly because it can lead to the introduction of noxious fish.

Small fish (not small trout) captured in the same waterway you are fishing are quite all right and will make good bait, particularly if fished live.

As a sidelight, frozen whitebait used in saltwater angling make very good trout bait on lakes where small fish are a major dietary item for the trout.

Food Blooms

Lakes sometimes experience 'food blooms' when conditions are ideal for a particular species to breed or hatch. Some of the obvious things are insect hatches of moths, mayflies, flying ants and black beetles. Mudeyes can occasionally do the same thing.

When these fall into the lake in huge numbers the trout will often feed on them exclusively.

The same thing can happen under the water with shrimps, yabbies and water fleas.

Good anglers are observant and note these natural food explosions and use baits, lures or flies to 'match the hatch' in fly-fishing language. By using something to simulate the preferred food of the trout, the chances of a hook-up are greatly increased.

This large brown trout fell to a yabby fished near the bottom.

MUDEYES — IRRESISTIBLE TO TROUT

Every fish has a weakness that can be exploited by anglers and when it comes to trout, that weakness is the mudeye.

The mudeye is the larval stage of the dragonfly, which is often seen hovering over the surface of ponds as it lays its eggs and catches small insects.

Mudeyes live in the water among the weeds, feeding voraciously on anything they can grab with their extended, pincered jaws.

While awaiting their metamorphosis into dragonflies, mudeyes live a very active life: feeding, growing and shedding their skins as they get bigger. Finally, when warm weather provides the stimulus, they crawl up out of the water to shed their skins for the final time and emerge as dragonflies.

Whether because of their taste and smell or because of their tantalising action, trout are very fond of mudeyes and actively feed on them at every opportunity.

Collecting Mudeyes

With mudeyes occurring in very limited numbers, fetching as much as $6 plus per dozen in the bait shops, most anglers try to collect their own.

Mudeyes are found all over Australia. Unfortunately, only a very few freshwater ponds provide the right environment. You may find several farm ponds almost next to each other, with only one of them having mudeyes present.

Mudeyes seem to like water which is reasonably clear, with a healthy weed growth, a big population of other types of organisms and not much interference from insecticides or fertilisers.

They can be collected with a small-meshed net pushed through the weed and along the bulrushes. The weed and rubbish that collect in the net should then be sorted out. It is best to put the weed back in the water, as it harbours the organisms that provide the food, as well as small mudeyes and eggs.

Gathering mudeyes is well worth the effort involved.

Collecting from Lakes

In lakes, mudeyes can sometimes be collected the same way. If the weed beds are absent, mudeyes can be collected by dragging dead timber to the edge and breaking it up with an axe. Mudeyes may be found in the crevices of this timber.

On large lakes, you can sometimes collect mudeyes by tying sugar bags into rolls and putting them into the shallows overnight. The next morning the mudeyes will be among the folds of the bags.

No matter how they are collected, it is hard work and usually involves much trial and error.

Storing Mudeyes

Once collected, perhaps the best container in which to store mudeyes is a small 'six pack' foam esky, which insulates them from the heat of the sun. For a short period of up to a couple of weeks, they can be kept in a little water and weed from the dam they were caught in.

If they get too warm, two things happen. Firstly, their metabolism speeds up and they begin to feed on each other, reducing their numbers, or, secondly, they crawl out of the water and start their transformation into dragonflies.

Should you need to keep them longer, they are best stored between layers of foam in the same small esky and placed in the vegetable section of a fridge. The cold of the fridge sends them into hibernation and they can be stored in a state of suspended animation for several months. When you come to use them they will appear dead, but after they thaw out, they soon start coming to life again.

Various Species of Mudeye

There are two main types of mudeyes used by anglers as bait, as well as several subspecies of the same type.

'Couta' mudeyes are long, canoe-shaped insects, while the 'bug' or 'spider' variety is, as the name suggests, short in body with long spindly legs.

In different locations, various subspecies exist which are slightly different in colour.

Along the Murray and in the warmer irrigation country, there exists a bright green couta mudeye which is particularly attractive to trout and makes a very good bait.

Fishing with Mudeyes

Mudeyes are usually either fished under floats (*see* **Bubble floats for trout**, p. 13) or trolled in conjunction with flasher-type attractors such as Cowbells, Ford Fenders and Bolos.

Apart from the standard float-fishing methods discussed previously, another method is mudeye 'dobbing'.

Mudeye dobbing is a time-tested method of float fishing which uses a fly-fishing outfit and floating line, but with a small piece of cork up the trace and a live mudeye in place of the fly. This mudeye is cast out alongside submerged timber and weeds, and gently jiggled, arousing the trout to strike. Often a slight ripple on the water provides enough movement for the float and mudeye to have the same effect.

All float-fishing methods used for mudeyes should be fished as close as possible to the kind of cover — such as weed beds and timber — where trout find their food. At times, this will mean fishing almost alongside the banks.

Trolling with Ford Fenders

Mudeyes can be trolled on a short trace behind a Ford Fender or similar attractor lure and in many lakes, such as Victoria's Lake Dartmouth, this technique is acknowledged as one of the most productive.

Both bug and couta mudeyes are used, with a long-shank hook being required for the couta mudeyes.

The hook point is inserted into the mudeye's head and then the insect's body is bent around the shank of the hook until the point comes out in the centre of the lower abdomen. The mudeye is then pulled up so that the entire knot and head of the hook disappears into the mudeye's head.

This provides a towing point in the front and prevents the mudeye from spinning, which it would do if it were resting on the bend of the hook.

The Ford Fender and mudeye is then fed back gently, about 35 m behind the boat, and trolled very slowly. Electric outboards with their slow, quiet trolling ability are often best for this method.

When trolled at this slow speed, the Ford Fender imparts a pulsating, bobbing motion to the mudeye, which is very similar to a free-swimming mudeye. The trout find this irresistible. Graphite rods are best for this trolling, as the bobbing action is also shown on the rod tip, letting you know that you are trolling at the right speed.

Other Approaches

All sorts of other methods are used with mudeyes, including fishing them on the bottom with a running sinker just like a bunch of worms, and lowering them down among the timber, allowing the wind to blow the boat to the other side of the clearing and then twitching the mudeyes back to the boat. No matter how they are used, mudeyes will catch trout.

Mudeyes are not only favoured by trout. Most native fish, including bass and Macquarie perch, love them, and imports like redfin cannot resist them either.

Without a doubt, mudeyes are the most effective all-round bait for trout, and well worth the time and trouble required to collect them.

A good catch of trout taken on mudeyes.

READING A RIVER

It matters very little whether you fish with bait, lures or flies; the ability to assess where the fish are to be found within a river or stream will have a marked impact on your catch.

Trout, like most river fish, will use the flow of water, the available cover, the time of day and particular feeding areas to provide themselves with food, protection and comfortable water temperatures.

River trout always face upstream when feeding and the fish expect their prey to be carried to them by the water flow. This means that generally baits, lures and flies work best when cast upstream and drawn back towards the angler.

From an angler's point of view, the aim is to place a bait, lure or fly where the fish are most likely to be looking for it.

When feeding, trout will use the top and bottom ends of pools. This applies particularly to the small to medium-sized fish. The head and tail of each pool are usually most productive in low light conditions of early morning or late afternoon. As the sun comes up the fish will tend to fall back into the deeper water.

If a major insect hatch happens during the day then the fish will respond to this by feeding on the surface, often carelessly. At this time they are easily seen by the angler.

As a rule, the fish usually don't feed in the rapids or fast-moving water between the pools.

During the main part of the day the fish tend to feed in the deeper water around weed beds, along deep banks or areas where bankside vegetation overhangs the water. Deep water along rock ledges is also a prime location.

The head and tail of any pool is always worth investigating as are any obstructions in the course of a river.

Trout will frequently take shelter under overhanging banks and ledges, particularly on bright or hot sunny days. They are more comfortable in shaded, cooler water than in hot, exposed areas.

Pools with areas of quiet water often hold fish. Occasionally the actual run-in point of the stream is not at the top of the pool but may be at the side, providing a still area away from the main run. These areas are ideal for bait fishing as trout will graze these areas looking for insect larvae and other bits and pieces.

Any object or formation that obstructs, juts into or changes the direction of water flow is always worth investigating. These 'pinches' in the stream or its flow will provide places for fish to feed.

In deeper streams, snags or trees that fall into the stream will regularly be adopted by big fish, usually brown trout. Working a bait, lure or fly around such a location may yield an exceptional fish.

In fast-running waters always look to areas that break up the flow of the stream. A big boulder right in the middle of the flow will provide an area of quiet water behind it. Fish will use this piece of quiet water as a holding station and a point to launch their attack out into the stream to grab passing prey. They then return to their protected spot.

These locations are usually worked with lures or flies rather than bait.

In fast-running streams any pockets of deep, quiet water are always likely to produce fish.

Places where small streams join larger streams or rivers are always worth investigating. Also, the first hole or pool upstream in the feeder creek may hold a good fish or two, even if it is a very small pool.

Streams can also vary in their character depending on the level of the water at the time. When the streams are swollen following heavy rain or snow melt, they may present a different picture to their normal flow.

When the streams are swollen or muddied, bait anglers usually do best working the quiet water in deeper holes as the fish will be pushed out of many of their usual feeding spots by the water volume coming downstream.

In discoloured water, baits are almost always the most productive.

Lure and fly anglers do best when stream flows are normal and the clear water gives the trout a good view of the lure or fly.

As can be seen, each piece of water needs careful analysis. The angler needs to look at each hole and run and assess its potential. The best catches always come by placing the bait, lure or fly where the fish are most likely to be lying.

Trout can often be spotted cruising a creek. You need polaroid sunglasses and a careful approach.

SPINCASTING FOR TROUT

Using light spincasting tackle to catch trout is a fun 'hunting' style of angling. It combines casting skills, streamcraft and fish-locating knowledge with the pleasure of walking along a stream or around a lake.

Most importantly, it is a very successful fishing method. It works on streams and lakes and it is relatively inexpensive.

While a great deal is written about fly fishing the streams, using spincasting gear is no different and usually allows the coverage of far more water than flycasting.

TACKLE

The real key to successful stream lure casting is to use tackle that is sensitive enough to cast the very light lures that are used in this type of angling.

The best rods are fine, medium to fast taper types with a single-handed grip. The rod should also be fairly short, less than 1.8 m, to assist in casting in tight corners.

Reels need to be small but of good quality to cope with the cast and retrieve routine used in spincasting. The reels also need a smooth drag system to play the fish on the light lines used.

The line should be around 3 kg breaking strain but you should selectively choose a line that is very fine for breaking strain with a diameter of 0.20 mm to 0.22 mm. This will assist in casting the lures but it is vital that the reel be kept topped up with line or casting distance will decline markedly.

Brown trout caught in the Snowy River near Jindabyne.

For anglers new to the sport, the sort of light rods used for estuary whiting and bream are a good start if you want to try using lures on trout without buying extra gear.

LURES

A small range of lures is all that is needed for both stream and lake spincasting.

Bladed lures are used extensively with the standard being about the size of a No. 2 Celta. However, any of the myriad bladed spinners on the market will work. The best colours to use are red, black and gold.

Small spoons and wobblers are used to gain casting distance where needed. These are very useful on long pools or on the lakes. When stream casting, stick to the smaller lure sizes but larger lures can be used on the lakes.

Small plugs and minnows are also very useful. Lures like the Rapala CD–5 in trout 'clone' colours or gold work well. Plugs like the tiny Rebel Crickhopper are also excellent when the trout are feeding on grasshoppers.

For casting around the shores of the lakes, very few lures are better than the Tassie Devil/Cobra types. These also cast well on an average spinning outfit, so they maximise the amount of water covered with the lure.

With a good outfit, the angler only needs polaroid sunglasses, six to ten lures in a pocket-sized tackle box, a dozen tiny snap swivels (black), a shoulder bag for the fish and a belt-attached landing net (optional). Waders are also recommended, particularly in alpine areas.

Tactics

In general it is always best to work a stream by walking and wading upriver. Trout feed facing upstream and they expect their prey to be carried down the river towards them. This is not always completely right and cross stream and downstream casting will also work.

The direction of the cast often depends on the geography of and access to the fishing location.

Streamcraft (*see* **Reading a river**, p. 22) is a vital part of spincasting. The angler selects the most promising-looking part of each pool and carefully works the lures by casting and retrieving.

The parts of the pool where water enters and leaves are always likely, as are deep undercut banks, the edges of weed beds and around snags.

By using polaroid sunglasses and a quiet, slow approach you can often see the trout cruising the pool, or a trout will reveal its location by taking an insect off the surface. Feeding trout are easily spooked by careless anglers who tramp along the water's edge without checking where the fish might be lying.

The lure should be cast past the fish's location and retrieved so that it passes in front of the fish. Having a lure crashing down on its nose will only scare the fish.

If the fish is feeding it will usually grab the lure with great relish and be hooked by the angler. Sometimes it may take a little coaxing and a quick change of lure often helps.

Trout that are rising to surface insects can sometimes ignore everything except the hatching or hovering insects. However, these rising fish can often be taken with a little perseverance.

Stream-dwelling trout feed very keenly and rarely reject an opportunity to grab an easy meal.

Lake Spinning

Casting lures around the shoreline of lakes can be productive. Often the casting is combined with a fair amount of walking but the method does catch fish. It is possible to cover a lot of water by just walking and casting in fan-shaped patterns to cover the area.

Lures that are heavy for body size and have a strong action work best for this type of fishing. These include Tassie Devils, Cobras, Pegron Tiger Minnows, Eucumbene Spoons and similar lures.

Trout can be pulled from a number of locations. Best results tend to come from deep shorelines or the points on the fingers of land that jut into the lake.

The lures work best when fished at varying depths. Often the lure is allowed to sink to the bottom before the retrieve starts. This brings the lure back through the water layers rather than just spinning the surface.

Lake spinning is usually at its best in the early morning or late in the afternoon. It takes care, attention to detail and a little perseverance but it does produce good fish.

Lure-caught brown trout about to be landed.

BASIC FLYCASTING

Artificial flies, especially those tied to imitate actual insects, are so light in weight that no ordinary fishing tackle could cast them. Real fly fishing demands that the fly is cast by means of a heavy, plastic-coated line specially made for the job.

Learning to make good use of this specialist tackle is the first hurdle beginner fly fishers must overcome. The actual fishing techniques take some mastering, but the very first, and perhaps the biggest, barrier to advancement is the requirement to cast a fly line.

GETTING STARTED

There are many 'how to' books on fly fishing which include casting instructions, and some excellent video cassettes. These are well worth studying, but nothing beats practice.

MATCH ROD STROKE TO LINE LENGTH

During casting, the rod is moved backwards and forwards. The distance the rod moves may be called the rod stroke. During the first portion of the stroke the rod straightens out the line and gets it moving in the desired direction. In the next portion of the stroke, increasing power is applied to bend the rod against the weight of the line. This is called loading the rod. At the end of the stroke, the loaded rod 'fires' the line.

When a short length of line is being cast, little rod management is required to straighten it out and get it moving. A long line, however, needs a longer stroke to accomplish these things. So too with the loading of the rod. The short line will not load the rod if the stroke is too long, while attempting to force too much into a short stroke will overload the rod.

The rule is quite simple: short lines require a short stroke and long lines a long stroke.

STOP HARD

If the loaded rod is to fire the line effectively, the rod must be stopped abruptly at the end of each stroke. The degree of rod loading depends on the weight of line being cast, the force being applied by the caster, and the speed with which this force is applied.

In every casting stroke, these factors will combine to produce a point when the rod is at its maximum loading for that particular cast. Once this point is past, the rod will begin to unload and throw the line, regardless of what the caster has planned.

This point of power transfer, when the

power stored in the rod during the loading portion of the stroke is transferred into the line, must be controlled by the caster. It is done by stopping the movement of the rod at the end of the stroke. Stopping hard is the best way to think of this, so that the stop is very deliberate, sudden and firm.

After the power transfer has occurred, the rod may be moved further in a follow-through, but the stop must be there first. This sudden stop is the thing which gives beginners most problems. It is necessary at the end of every stroke, both backwards and forwards.

Apply Power Smoothly

Many casting problems are caused when force is applied too early in the stroke or in a jerky fashion. Beginners who are used to casting light, single-handed spinning rods have most difficulty with this. To make a forward cast, they tend to start the rod forward too suddenly, putting all the power into the beginning of the stroke. The result is the classic 'buggy whip' cast, often snapping off the fly.

Each rod stroke must be started relatively slowly, so that there is a smooth build-up of speed and force culminating in the hard stop. Only in this way can the stop coincide with the point of maximum rod loading. In other words, the caster controls the moment of power transfer.

Maintain a Firm Wrist

It is difficult to apply force smoothly and at the right time if there is much wrist movement. When casting a short line, there should be a short stroke, and a relatively small force should be applied with great speed. Most people achieve this with a snap of the wrist and little movement of the arm. This works up to a point.

Making casts of 10 or 12 m — a pretty normal distance — it is essential that most of the rod stroke is made with an arm movement. Trying to make such casts with the sort of wristy action often seen results not only in poor casts, but in a sore wrist at the end of the day.

Beginners are well advised to concentrate on keeping their wrist firm while stroking the rod back and forth. A well-balanced stance with feet apart will allow the caster to loosen up the arm, shoulder, and upper body to produce a smooth flowing stroke. A firm grip on the rod and a firm wrist are essential for smooth power and hard stops.

Where the Hand Goes, the Line Goes

If the upper arm is held still while the hand pivots around the elbow joint, or worse still if the whole arm is held rigid while the hand pivots at the wrist, the rod tip will tend to move in an arc just as the hand is doing. The line must follow the rod tip, so it will also move through the air in an arc, producing graceful open loops which do not make good casts.

In false casting, the intention is that the line should speed back and forth, making tight casting loops which assist maximum transfer of power and stay parallel to the ground.

For this to happen, the rod tip must move in straight lines, not arcs. Correctly loading the rod helps achieve this, but the caster must also move the rod back and forth in straight lines. False casting is done with the hand making push and pull movements with the rod. The hand should be kept up at about shoulder level, and the whole arm, shoulder, and upper body will move to accommodate these movements.

Picking up line from the water, throwing a high back cast, then delivering a forward cast requires a different trajectory of the hand. The hand should still move in straight lines, but now it will be a line from just above waist level in front to shoulder level or even up beside the ear of the caster. The hand will then push straight forward for a false cast, or in a line sloping down for a delivery. This action is used for representing a fly without having to go through the action of repeated back casting.

When casting for distance, the delivery needs to be aimed high. The hand should therefore describe a straight line tipped up at the front.

Follow through this idea, and it will become easy to make the line go wherever it is desired. High back casts are no longer a problem, and neither are low ones when it is necessary to stay beneath overhanging trees.

A fat rainbow trout caught on flycasting gear.

TROUT FLIES

Fly fishing is regarded by some pundits as daunting and almost mystical. In reality, it is just another fishing technique — one that's best tackled by looking first at the business end of the rig: the fly itself.

The technique of presenting an artificial fly to fish so that it imitates a natural insect appears to have originated in Europe where trout are one of the most sought-after freshwater fish.

In the past, freshwater fly fishing was often considered the domain of the privileged. This misconception prevented many people from trying a sport which offers great challenges, rewards and pleasure.

The main difference between true flycasting and other kinds of fishing relates to the weight of the flies. Because they are so light — most weighing only a fraction of a gram — a heavy line is required to make the rod flex and store energy during the casting action. It is the line that is cast rather than the fly itself.

Built Around Trout

Other differences relate to the behaviour and feeding pattern of trout: the group of fish for which fly fishing was developed.

Trout feed mainly by sight rather than smell. They prefer clear streams in which they can easily locate their food and observe intruders. For this reason, fly anglers must develop the art of stalking fish if they are to be successful.

Feathers, Fur and Tinsel

Basically, a freshwater fly is a hook, covered with a number of materials tied in such a way as to deceive a fish into believing it to be its natural food. It can resemble an insect or other small organism swimming or resting on the surface of the water or somewhere in the water column.

Besides insects, flies are also tied to resemble tadpoles, mudeyes, nymphs, small fish, shrimps and the like.

Materials

Artificial flies are constructed of various kinds of materials such as feathers, hair, fur and tinsel which are bound onto the hook and tied with thread or silk. These replicas may be bought at tackle outlets or made by the angler, with the necessary equipment.

Basically, for freshwater fishing, there are two types of flies: dry flies which float and wet flies which sink, although there are several categories within these broad headings.

Some flies don't closely represent any particular creature. They are designed simply to arouse the instincts of a fish. These patterns are sometimes called 'suggesters'.

Dry Flies

A dry fly is designed to float on top of the water or within the surface film. This is achieved by using materials that are as light and buoyant as possible. Often the finished artificial is also dipped or sprayed with a water-repellent material to keep it afloat.

The dry fly is traditionally fished with a floating fly line and a greased or floating leader. It is fished in such a way as to float downstream at precisely the same speed as the current. Some dry flies have been designed to imitate the movement of beetles or grasshoppers which have fallen onto the surface of the water and are trying to escape. Action is imparted by the angler.

Most dry flies, however, are replicas of the aquatic insects which are the main item on a stream trout's menu. The most important of these are the mayflies, damselflies, caddis flies and, to a lesser extent, the stoneflies, crane flies and dragonflies. All trout eat these insects at various stages of their life cycles.

Of all these insects, the mayflies are of prime interest to the angler. The small, slow-flowing weedy streams of the Australian highland plateaus have a rich variety of mayflies, some of which produce enormous hatches which bring trout to the surface in search of a meal.

Successful Imitations

Especially in the small streams around the border between New South Wales and Victoria, imitations of mayflies are the most used and most successful dry flies.

For the angler who wants to go fishing in the evening, the caddis flies are extremely valuable. Some of the best fishing during the months of daylight saving can occur when these insects are prevalent.

Sometimes known to anglers as 'moths', the most common caddis fly is the white, but there are also a number of grey, brown and darker varieties.

The artificial called a Hairwing Coachman is an excellent replica of the lighter caddis flies. There are also other suitable patterns which imitate the darker moths.

Dry Fly Technique

Once an angler is beside the stream the technique used can make all the difference between success and failure. In small streams dry fly fishing demands accurate casting. Long-distance casting is not required, but landing the fly lightly on the water in the right spot is essential, as is the avoidance of unnatural 'drag' on the fly line.

Technique depends on the nature of the stream flow. The dry fly angler usually fishes upstream because trout face into the current. Facing upstream ensures that food is swept down to the fish by the current.

Nymph Fishing

There are certain times when trout feed almost exclusively on nymphs, which are the immature underwater stage of aquatic insects. Nymph fishing involves casting a small fly upstream or across the flow so that it drifts down to the fish beneath the surface.

The nymph is a sinking fly, so it falls

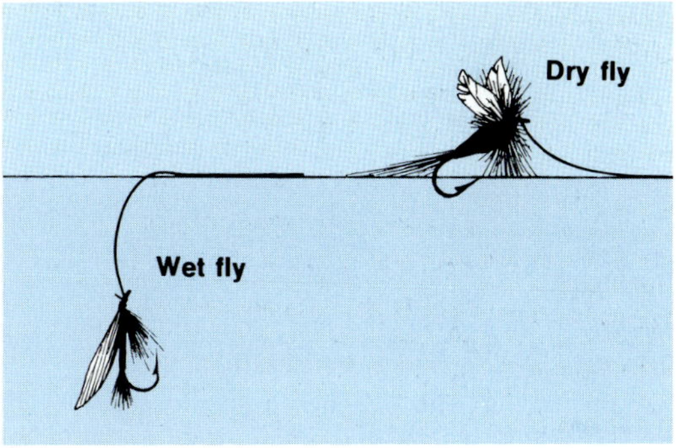

Flies are designed as either wet fly or dry fly. One to sink, the other to float. The wet fly should resemble a drowning insect or aquatic creature. The dry fly is meant to depict a moth, butterfly or other insect that has landed on the surface.

into the general category of 'wet flies'. However, it is fished more in the manner of a dry fly — upstream or across and down on a floating line and often with a partially greased leader, leaving the fly suspended only 10 or 20 cm under the water.

Most nymphs are constructed to imitate the larvae of the mayfly or caddis fly, which make up the bulk of a trout's diet. When trout show a preference for nymphs, a Seal's Fur artificial fished on a 3 m leader can be beneficial in interesting the fish. If trout are feeding close to the surface, a gold-ribbed Hare's Ear or a hatching nymph pattern can also work.

Another way of arousing the trout's interest is to attach a small piece of fluffy feather to the sides of the nymph with gold or copper ribbing. The slightest movement will cause those fluffy fibres to imitate the struggles of the nymph, and will often attract the trout.

Wet Flies

Wet flies are, as the name suggests, designed to sink rather than float. Many patterns can be tied in both dry and wet versions. The well-known dry fly called a Coachman, which is a replica of the white-winged caddis, also has an appropriate wet version. The 'wet' Coachman is tied with softer absorbent hen's hackle which permits it to sink.

There are some streams where the water is so turbulent due to rapids or small waterfalls that any insect landing on the surface will soon be drowned. In these situations, the fish's food will be taken at lower depths, so a wet fly is more appropriate.

Quite often wet flies are not constructed to represent any particular insect but are designed to interest, annoy or excite the fish into striking. This approach is particularly successful in larger bodies of water, and is widely used by anglers fishing lakes.

Wet flies can also be very effective after dark. In this situation, the retrieve should be varied: on some occasions the fish will take a fly when it's moving very, very slowly, whereas at other times only a quick, jerky action will provoke a strike or take.

Successful Patterns

Some proven wet flies include the Black and Red Matuka, Mrs Simpson, Hammil Killers, Craig's Night Time and the Muddler Minnow patterns.

During the summer months, fish leave the shallows and head for the cooler, deeper water.

During these times, select a place on the shore where the lake bed drops off quickly or use a boat to strategically place your cast in deeper water.

A nymph or wet fly may be fished down as far as 30 m by using a sinking line or by placing some very small split shot on the leader or using lead wire in the body of the fly.

The angler should keep experimenting with varying depths until successful, as fish often change their position depending on the water temperature.

A selection of dry flies suitable for use on Australian streams and impoundments.

FRESHWATER DOWNRIGGING

The future for freshwater downrigging in Australia lies in our large dams and impoundments. All big dams exhibit conditions at various times of the year where the trout — and to a lesser extent natives — move vertically and inhabit the depths for considerable periods of time.

The main reason for this is that during hotter months inland lake water becomes distinctly stratified into three separate layers — the top or epilimnion, the middle or thermocline and the bottom layer or hypolimnion. The top layer, epilimnion, is usually quite warm, and can extend down to a fair depth in hot months. Although there is plenty of oxygen in this layer, the salmonoids find the higher temperature most uncomfortable, and will only stay in this layer for short periods of time, usually around dawn or dusk.

The middle layer is the compressed thermocline. This is the area that the downrigger angler looks for as it has a regime of water temperature and oxygen content best suited to the trout. Here the water is noticeably cooler than the top layer, and yet still retains high levels of oxygen. Often the thermocline layer can be quite compressed over the hot months. The thermocline can be detected with quality echo sounders and with this knowledge you know how deep to set your lures.

Below the thermocline lies the hypolimnion — a layer of water far cooler than either of the other two — but as it often has very low levels of dissolved oxygen it can be most unattractive to the fish.

This classic scenario of stratification can last for many months, and it's usually not until the first cold of winter along with the windy weather that there is some intermixing and break-up of the layers. Aided in this mixing is the 'sink effect', whereby the winter cools the surface layer, making it more dense, causing it to 'sink' and merge with the thermocline, and eventually the hypolimnion.

So, as one can see, the position where a salmonoid may be in a lake at any time of the year can be quite difficult to predict. There are a few general rules to go by, however.

Over summer, look at the thermocline during the day, and the shallows at dawn and dusk. During winter the situation can be a bit tricky, as the general regime of the lake has improved significantly, and the fish could be found at any level, including right down near the bottom.

What should a prospective lake troller learn from this? Well, the first fact is that a downrigger can be equally useful in summer or winter. In summer, target the thermocline, but in winter, have a good look at all levels.

GETTING DOWN TO BUSINESS

The simplest way to start downrigger fishing is just to use one rod and one lure per downrigger. A suitable release mechanism or release clip is attached to the 'bomb' or downrigger trolling weight via a short length of game wire (30 m), the lure is run out behind the boat to the desired distance and the line is then clipped into the release. Next, the drag on the reel is backed off — or better still if using a baitcaster 'click on' the ratchet with the reel in free spool — and the bomb is lowered slowly, pulling the line evenly off the reel as it goes.

When the depth of the bomb is set, the reel should be set in gear with a moderate drag and the rod should be loaded against the downrigger weight to about 90 degrees. Often the first indication of a strike is a wobble of the rod tip.

Ideally, downrigger rods should have a medium taper action. Level-wind baitcasters have long been the best choice for downrigging reels, as long as they have a 'click' or ratchet incorporated in their design.

INCREASING THE SPREAD

Going up from the single rod and single

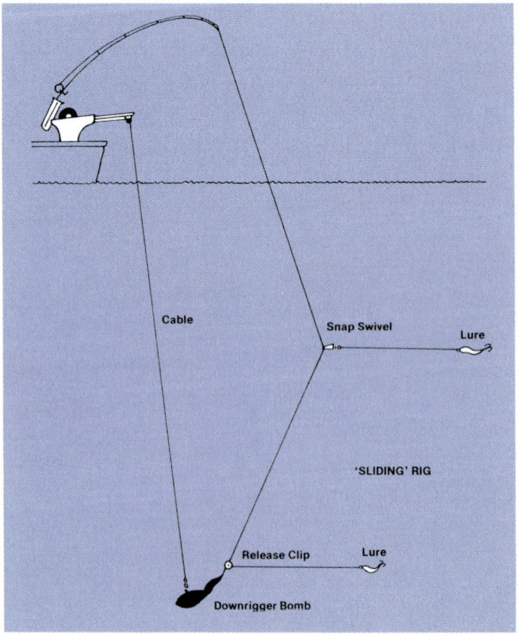

The 'slider' rig allows a second lure or bait to be deployed off one line. Firstly, a rig is deployed as usual in the downrigger release clip and lowered to the desired depth. Next, a trace of some 1 to 3 m is made up with a lure or bait at one end and a quality snap swivel at the other end. This swivel is snapped onto the line from the outfit in the rigger and allowed to slide down. It will stop almost exactly halfway to the first lure because of the belly in the line generated by water drag.

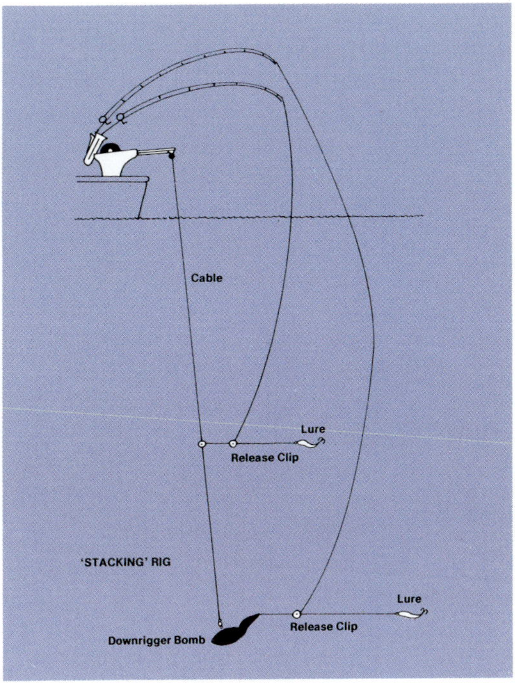

The 'stacker' rig employs a single downrigger and bomb to fish two lures or baits from two separate outfits. To do this, a second release clip must be rigged on the cable at a predetermined distance above the bomb. The first line is clipped into the standard release at the bomb and lowered away. When the desired position for the second line is reached, the second release clip is attached, the line put in place, and this rig also lowered away. To avoid tangles, set-back distances on both rigs should be different.

lure system, you can keep adding lures, even extra rods, to the system. The easiest addition to start with though is what is called a 'slider'. This is simply a short length of monofilament with a lure at one end and a good-quality snap swivel at the other.

This enables two lures to be trolled off the one rod, but at two different depths. Simply set the bottom lure off the bomb at the desired depth, and then clip the snap onto the line near the tip of the rod and throw the lure overboard. This rig will then slide down the line and take up a position midway between the rod tip and the bomb (see diagram p.36).

Some anglers use two and even three rods off the one downrigger. To do this you must employ a system called 'stacking'. Here the heart of the principle is achieved by using dual release clips: one to clip onto the downrigger wire and the other to attach the line (see diagram above).

Using two or more rods requires a bit of organising and coordination but nonetheless can be achieved and executed easily with practice.

Some other guidelines of importance to downrigging newcomers are the distances behind the bomb one should troll the lure. To prevent tangles it is always best to have mid-range stackers up short so they can't tangle with the trailing belly of the deep set rods. Additionally, there is a general rule that the deeper the lure the closer the trail-back length behind the bomb. This is because it is known that a lot of fish actually come up and inspect the bomb, hence it is quite advantageous to have the lure trailing only some 4 to 5 m behind.

Downrigger Lures

There are thousands of different types of lures available to the downrigger angler.

Unfortunately, most have never seen the Australian market. We have, however, a number of imported and locally produced lures that are particularly effective when used on downriggers. Tillins, King Cobras, Pegrons, Tobys, Crocodile Spoons, Wigstons, Rapalas, Yo-Zuris, Nilsmasters and more have all been successful on the downrigger for trout.

The last area that prospective downrigger anglers should become acquainted with is attractors. Cowbells and Ford Fenders have been long used in Australia, but these are only the tip of the iceberg.

These rotating-blade attractors are great at attracting trout. An alternative is to use what is called a Dodger — a large chrome or painted spoon-type attractor that 'wobbles' through the water rather than spins. These are great fish attractors and work well on deep trolling gear.

Downrigging in freshwater is thinking vertically and adjusting accordingly. It will require cooperation between all parties on the boat, but once a system of lowering the bombs and lures is accomplished the scene becomes much easier.

The main thing to remember when downrigging is to know your depth, have your tackle organised and keep the boat in gear going forward, even when a fish is on.

Most trout can be brought up the back of the boat without having to retrieve or pull up the other bombs. Remember, though, that a boat drifting backward over its set of downriggers and lines will result in a tangle that defies comprehension.

MURRAY COD

The largest and most important of Australia's freshwater fish and one of the biggest freshwater species in the world, the Murray cod offers inland anglers some great sport and superb eating.

The Murray cod is not related to the true cod — a saltwater fish of the northern hemisphere — but is, in fact, a member of the Serranidae family which includes a number of freshwater perch and the Australian bass.

The Murray cod was once found in nearly all parts of the Murray–Darling river system, which comprises a large number of important rivers in New South Wales, Victoria and Queensland.

In the early years of outback settlement, specimens were taken from many different points and transferred to new locations: mainly dams and other river systems, but also interstate to waters as far away as Albany in Western Australia.

A Comeback for the Cod

Ten years ago there were serious doubts in some circles that the Murray cod would survive as a species. Victims of an altered natural habitat and over-harvesting, cod numbers had dwindled dramatically since the Second World War.

Although Murray cod fishing may never return to the good old days, recent statistics show that the fish has made something of a comeback and is now at least holding its own, with reasonable to good populations present in many areas.

Profile of an Outback Brawler

The Murray cod is a powerfully built fish with a deep, rounded body. In exceptional instances it grows to a length of nearly 2 m and weights of 100 kg, although specimens larger than 40 kg are rare these days.

The cod has a large mouth and a big, rounded tail. Its colour is generally creamy yellow on the flanks with a greenish-brown back and pale cream belly. It is covered on the back and sides with mottled dark green to black blotches. The dorsal and caudal fins are covered with dark green spots and markings, and in clearer water the fins display clean, white margins.

The Breeding Cycle

Spawning is usually stimulated by a rise in the water level combined with a rise in water temperature. It usually takes place in late spring or early summer.

The fish may move upstream against floodwaters prior to spawning and this upstream movement is well known and eagerly awaited by local cod fanciers along the major inland rivers.

Home Among the Snags

Murray cod occur in some swiftly moving waters, but generally they prefer warm, sluggish sections of a river. They often make their home in the deeper holes where they can take cover in or around hollow logs, among drowned trees and near large, semi-submerged rocks and boulders.

Any natural obstruction to the water flow is a likely Murray cod hang-out. As well as the obvious snag and log spots, areas close to outward bends of the river where the current has cut into the clay banks are good for prospecting. These clay banks offer shelter for the fish and are usually loaded with yabbies and other natural food.

Murray cod are most active in summer, especially at night. During daylight they usually shelter near submerged logs or rocks and take up a position where the current and back eddies will bring food to them.

The cod displays lightning-fast speeds over short distances, enabling it to catch even quick-swimming prey.

Boating is Best

While it's possible for riverbank anglers to take good catches, the best fishing is usually accessed by boat.

The choice of boat is important. The craft needs to be easily handled and capable of getting right in among the snags which represent typical cod country.

While anything up to a houseboat can be used on inland rivers and dams, an aluminium dinghy with a small to medium outboard motor is ideal for cod fishing.

Watch the Barometer

Atmospheric pressure can play a big part in hooking a cod, and most regular anglers like the air pressure to be quite high. When clouds gather and the weather is building towards a thunderstorm after a hot, still day, cod often turn on a real spurt of activity.

Tackle for Cod

The best cod territory consists of a mass of sunken trees, sharp rocks and other obstacles conducive to broken lines and lost lures. Inland streams can be very hard on tackle and in the course of a day's fishing, it's not unlikely that you may sacrifice a fair amount of terminal tackle.

Six kilo breaking strain line is considered light tackle for Murray cod in most areas, and if you're after a big one, you'll need 10 kg plus tackle in the majority of locations.

Murray cod are a handsome and prized sportfish.

While more traditional outback anglers may opt for a handline or a set line, sport anglers prefer a baitcaster or medium weight threadline outfit, especially for lure casting and trolling, though the same gear is ideally suited to bait fishing as well.

Accurate Casting

Long casting is not usually required when cod fishing. Accuracy in dropping your bait or lure onto the edge of a likely hole or snag is more important, but beware of the current which will quickly drag your line around and snag it. On some days, you may need to go from pool to pool along a given stretch of the river or drift from snag to snag if boat fishing. This will increase your chances of taking home a cod. It's often futile to keep casting a bait in one area when the fish are in holes elsewhere.

Baits and Feeding

Murray cod are voracious eaters and feed on virtually anything smaller than themselves, including other fish, yabbies, shrimps, mussels, water birds, water rats, lizards, frogs, grubs and worms.

A favoured bait is a large, lively tiger or red worm which will take cod up to 3 kg and more.

Many Murray River anglers believe the best bait of all to be the bardie grub: the large, juicy larvae of a giant moth which is found in the ground under the limbs of red gum and yellow box trees along the riverbanks.

For those not keen on collecting these grubs, supplies can sometimes be bought at local towns near cod fishing waters.

The cod can also be enticed by a bait of shrimp but not many really big specimens are caught this way. On the other hand, a big yabby — crushed to allow a flow of juices — will often attract a large cod.

Bites on Baits

When a cod peruses a bait, attracted by the smell or vibrations, it observes it for a few moments before striking. When it decides to bite, it does so with a quick lunge and takes the offering completely into its mouth with a lightning-fast movement and snap of those cavernous jaws. The cod may then turn the bait around in its large mouth before swallowing it, especially if the offering is a live fish.

It is during this second action that the fish will fall victim to a nicely presented hook. Many anglers miss hooking a Murray cod by not allowing the fish a little slack line after first registering a take.

If you strike too soon, the hook is likely to miss sinking into the hard mouth parts of the fish. Let the bait go a little deeper and a hook-up is almost assured, for although the cod has a large mouth, it's very much a one-way passage: everything slides in easily but doesn't always come out as readily.

Cod on Lures

The Murray cod is very susceptible to a well-presented lure. Dams and inland lakes are good spots to try lures on cod, especially through the period between October and May when the fish are particularly active. Working the backwater areas near drowned timber will bring the best results.

Outback rivers also provide fine lure casting and trolling, particularly on those relatively rare occasions when the water runs clear.

The aeroplane spinner and flatfish are two evergreen favourites with cod anglers, though nowadays anglers have a very wide selection of imported and locally produced lure ranges from which to select their cod plugs.

These include Boomerangs, Stumpjumpers, Storm Hot'N'Tots, Hellbenders, Rebels, Bennet McCraths, Newells and the like.

As for lure colours, bright fluorescent yellows and reds are best in dirty water, while more natural brown and green hues work best in clearer conditions.

Most cod anglers who use lures also agree that late in the afternoon until darkness falls is the best time to take the bigger cod, although they can be taken at any time.

Good Eating

The Murray cod is rated as one of the best-eating freshwater fish in the country. It has a distinctive flavour, a tender flaky flesh and adapts well to a wide variety of fish recipes.

Its firm, white fillets or steaks may be poached, cooked in soup, fried in butter or coated with crumbs and fried in hot oil. Many prefer smaller fish to be stuffed and baked.

To make the most of the fish's superb flesh quality, kill the cod by cutting its throat with a sharp knife as soon as it's taken from the river. It should then be gutted, cleaned and all blood carefully removed from the spine. Where possible, leave the freshly caught fish in the refrigerator overnight before skinning.

Because of the layer of fat found between the skin and the flesh of the Murray cod, some people consider the fish too fatty for frying. This can be overcome by removing the unwanted fat. Simply skin the fish and scrape away the fatty layer with a knife. The problem is reduced by eating only smaller, leaner fish and releasing the heavyweights.

The head of a big old cod preserved as a trophy.

GOLDEN PERCH

One of the most important fish of our outback and inland rivers, the golden perch (*Macquaria ambigua*), also known as yellowbelly, callop and Murray perch, makes a great contribution to the sport of inland anglers, responding to a variety of baits and lures and putting up a good fight. In addition, it provides an excellent meal.

Golden perch are widely distributed through the Murray–Darling river system, including most dams west of the Great Dividing Range. They are also found in the eastern-flowing Dawson River of central Queensland and the Bulloo, Lake Eyre and Coopers Creek drainage systems. However, as a result of extensive breeding and stocking in recent years, the golden perch has been introduced into many other parts of inland Australia.

Hump-shouldered Predator

Like other species belonging to the same taxonomic group, the golden perch is a deep-bodied fish with a solid muscular appearance. Older specimens have a conspicuous lower jaw and the wrist of the tail is thick, strong and rounded. Males tend to have a more evenly balanced shape and do not grow to the same dimensions as the females, which develop a noticeably hump-shouldered appearance.

Mature females often appear to have a head that is too small for their body; their body width is often equal to their length from snout to tail. This is particularly apparent in larger specimens.

The golden perch can grow to weights well in excess of 10 kg; however, most catches these days weigh between 0.5 and 3 kg.

Varied Colouration

The body colour of these fish is usually related to the colour of the waters they inhabit. In the muddy rivers of the plains country of western New South Wales, Queensland and South Australia, golden perch take on a very light cream, yellow or beige colour, with darker spots or mottling.

In clearer waters, the back of the fish may be olive green, lightening to a bluish tinge in fish from semi-clear rivers and dams. Fish that have lived for some time in clear water develop a deep, golden belly area.

Spawning is influenced by water temperatures and rises in water levels. Fish populations move considerable distances upstream when flooding occurs, and spawning takes place when water temperatures are between 23° and 26°C.

Spawning usually takes place at night in spring and summer. Larvae swim actively and start feeding on plankton about five days after spawning.

Survival Capacity

Although golden perch inhabit a variety of river environments, these fish seem to prefer warmer, turbid, sluggish streams. However, the fish have wide physiological tolerances, being able to withstand a range of temperatures from 4° to 37°C. Given the harsh conditions of the Australian inland, these native fish show a remarkable capacity for survival.

When the waters dry up during droughts, there are high mortality rates and increased competition for food. However, when the rains finally arrive, the relatively few fish that have survived are able to quickly restore former populations. In a single spawning, a female yellowbelly releases more than half a million eggs.

The Onslaught of 'Civilisation'

In spite of this, the fish have not done well in those areas where fertile soil has resulted in intensive land cultivation. Siltation and pollution due to pesticides are among the major factors which have reduced populations of golden perch.

The main cause of decline through their natural range has been the construction of weirs, reservoirs and locks on the major river systems. These structures impede the natural migration of the fish. Moreover, this regulation of rivers reduces the incidence of flooding, and the lower temperature of water released from these impoundments limits the fish's ability to breed.

Long-distance Travellers

Tagging has shown that golden perch are able to undertake remarkable long-distance migrations. A fish tagged after being captured from the Murray River below Euston was recovered months later and 350 km away near Leeton. Another tagged specimen released in the Murray River in South Australia was recovered years later 2000 km upstream in Queensland, in a tributary of the Darling River!

Feeding Habits

The diet of golden perch consists mainly of crustaceans, aquatic insect larvae and molluscs. Small fish such as goldfish and European carp also make up part of its diet in some streams. These feeding habits more or less confine them to the lower part of the water column layers and the bottom or bed of the river.

Golden perch feed both during the day and at night. As far as angling is concerned, the fish can be regarded as a bottom dweller, although it is known that they move into shallow water when feeding at night.

During periods of flooding, the fish will feed on miscellaneous matter that is forced from the ground.

Other fish cruise very slowly over weed beds, sandbanks and pebbly spots and will often burrow their noses into crevices and weed beds in search of suitable food items. They have also occasionally been seen rising to the surface, almost trout-like, to take live grasshoppers.

Shrimp and Yabby Baits

The most popular baits for yellowbelly include whole yabbies or yabby tails, shrimps, grubs, mudeyes and worms. Baits of live shrimps are a favourite with many inland anglers. These are usually suspended about 30 cm above the bottom, fished either under a float or with a dropper rig and worked around drowned trees, edges of weed beds, undercut banks and rocky drop-offs.

Some anglers prefer to rig their line with a light sinker and place their bait right on the bottom. This technique will take fish but it can also snag easily. Often golden perch choose a certain water depth and remain there in spite of tempting morsels placed above or below, so varying depths should be tried until a hook-up or two is achieved.

Another popular technique with baits is 'bobbing'. The bait is bounced up and down on the bottom with the aid of a heavy sinker, the commotion serving to attract them to the bait.

Golden perch are a common and popular inland capture.

Lures in Clear Water

In relatively clear water, golden perch can be readily taken with a wide range of spinners, spoons and plugs.

The typical inland technique for working a lure slow and deep is usually successful. Casting at areas of logs, rock bars, weed beds and other cover or 'structure' will bring the best results.

Where the water is murky in far-western rivers, lures are not widely used as the fish can't easily see or find them. However, a number of deeper holes which have cleared due to long periods of dry weather can often produce fish, especially when rain creates a slightly milky flow of water into the pool. Small minnow and yabby-type lures are often successful.

When the water level is really low, the fish are not usually too active. However, when there is a substantial rise in the river level, anglers should concentrate on locations where fish movement is obvious. The junctions of rivers and creeks and those spots which represent a barrier to upstream movement can suddenly become real hot spots.

Unpredictable Biters

Many members of the cod and perch family have the reputation of being 'moody' biters. During one outing they will bite well, but next time out, they can't be tempted. Similarly there will be no action in the morning, then suddenly during the afternoon, one hook-up follows the other.

Generally, yellowbelly bite best during spring and autumn and are somewhat sluggish through winter. However, as soon as a river is replenished with fresh rains, the fish will come on the bite.

Baits and lures should be fished fairly deep in the middle of the day and often the best results will be achieved from dusk until a couple of hours after dark. Anglers will also achieve better results if they adopt a hunter rather than a trapper approach to taking this fish. Lighter lines, lures, sport-fishing techniques and a mobile approach will all benefit the angler.

Handle with Care

Golden perch have some physical features that can injure careless anglers. The spines on the dorsal and anal fins become erect when the fish is taken from the water. A cut from these fins can inflict a painful wound that may become septic if left unattended.

Also, the gill cover has a razor-sharp cutting edge that can badly gash a thumb in the wrong position. To avoid these hazards, the fish should be held upright and its lower jaw clamped between thumb and forefinger. This will keep the fish relatively subdued and allow hooks and lures to be removed without risk of injury.

Firm White Flesh

The golden perch is rated as one of Australia's best-eating freshwater fish. The flesh is firm, white and succulent. Larger fish are likely to be lined with fat and as much of this as possible should be trimmed off, particularly along the back line adjacent to the stomach. If the fillets are grilled, the remaining fat will be lost in the cooking process.

If not overcooked, the fish will remain moist and well textured. Like most freshwater fish, golden perch can sometimes have a slightly 'muddy' taint. This is particularly evident in larger specimens taken from turbid waters. Home chefs can overcome this slight taint by the addition of a lightly spiced sauce to the cooked fish.

The flesh is excellent for barbecues, smoking, grilling, frying, mornay and sweet-and-sour dishes. The bones are easily removed which makes it a good fish to serve to small children.

SILVER PERCH

Depending upon location, the silver perch (*Bidyanus bidyanus*) is variously known as black bream, Murray bream, grunter, bidyan, Murray perch and bidyan grunter.

The silver perch is one of a large group of fish which belong to the grunter family. Many of these fish emit a characteristic 'grunt', produced by the vibration of the swim bladder, as they are taken from the water.

Range

Silver perch are extremely widespread, with a range that extends through much of the Murray–Darling river system, parts of the Coopers Creek–Lake Eyre drainage and a handful of coastal, flowing streams in New South Wales and Queensland.

All the tributaries of the Murray, Murrumbidgee, Lachlan and Darling Rivers, as well as the Barwon, Namoi, Macquarie and Gwydir Rivers, hold good numbers of silver perch.

The fish have also been widely stocked in major impoundments, lakes and farm dams through southern Queensland, New South Wales, Victoria and parts of eastern South Australia. Probably some of the best concentrations of fish can now be found in dams such as Windamere near Mudgee and Burrinjuck on the Murrumbidgee River.

Ability to Acclimatise

Silver perch are the ideal fish for stocking farm dams, as they eat both plant and animal material. Large numbers have been bred in hatcheries and sold to farmers for this purpose, while other stocks have been introduced to dams and lakes including Lake Burley Griffin in Canberra.

Perch-like Appearance

The silver perch has those characteristics associated with most fish called 'perch'. The most distinctive features are its relatively small head, a humped appearance and a scalloped dorsal fin with twelve spines. Its tail is slightly concave when spread flat.

On larger specimens, this humped look gives the impression that the fish's head is too small for its body. Fish around 1 kg and less have a more streamlined appearance.

Other characteristics include a small mouth, sharp spines and gill covers which can inflict a painful wound if care is not taken when handling the fish. Overall colour is usually silvery grey, darker on the upper body and fading to lighter tones underneath.

Darker, almost black, specimens of silver perch occur in clearer streams and lighter coloured fish are generally found in more cloudy waters. The fish has fine, diamond-shaped scales which are arranged symmetrically, giving the fish a beautiful netted appearance.

Baits and Lures

The silver perch shows enthusiasm for natural baits such as shrimps, small yabbies, worms, insects and grubs. The fish also eats vegetable matter such as zooplankton, algae and aquatic plants.

A small lure worked deep will often bring results, though feeding fish will move off the bottom and hunt in mid-water, where the fish will grab baits and lures while they are still sinking. In fact, silver perch are one of the few native freshwater fish that will feed on the surface. Grasshoppers and other insects that land on the surface are a top prey for silver perch.

On hot afternoons and evenings, anglers fishing the shallow mudflats of Burrinjuck Dam have reported encountering a mass of winged insects hovering near the surface of the water. When these conditions prevail, silver perch come on the bite, feeding on the surface for these tasty morsels and snapping up any 'dive bomber' that falls into their territory.

Aggressive Feeders

Lure anglers in search of silver perch should try small bladed spinners or spoons. Silver perch will also fall to a number of trout flies such as Mrs Simpson, Fuzzy Wuzzy and Hamill's Killer, as well as little plugs and minnows.

During the warmer months of the year when the fish are spawning and feeding a lot more aggressively, silver perch have been known to attack larger lures. However, these fish have small mouths, so lures should be selected accordingly.

Although the silver perch is known to grow to 7 kg, a catch of that weight would be considered exceptional. Generally speaking, most fish landed are between 200 g and 1 kg, with a 2 kg catch considered a very good fish.

Except in specific areas, such as Windamere and Burrinjuck Dams where there are known good stocks of silver perch, not many inland anglers specifically target these fish. Most are captured by anglers chasing trout, golden perch or Murray cod. However, once a hook-up has been achieved, many anglers are delighted at the performance of these strong fighters.

Dry White Flesh

Although good eating, the fish's flesh is dry and sometimes a little 'weedy' in comparison with Murray cod and golden perch, and many people only find the meal appealing if the chef prepares the fish with an appetising sauce or uses other ingredients that can compensate for the dryness. Silver perch is reasonably well suited to smoking.

MACQUARIE PERCH

Confined to the rivers, streams and dams of south-eastern Australia, the Macquarie perch is one of our top freshwater angling species, providing excellent sport and superb table fare for inland anglers.

This fish is sometimes referred to as mountain perch, indicating the preference for the higher altitude streams of the Murray–Darling river system. In other areas it is known as the white-eye or silver-eye.

Along with other native fish, the Macquarie perch has suffered from the destruction of its habitat, man-made pollution and competition from introduced species such as carp and redfin.

The Macquarie perch is actually a member of the bass family. It has a prominent lateral line and a thick, powerful body which slopes sharply from the shoulder to the head, giving it a humped appearance, characteristic of several native perches.

It has strong fins and a thick, powerful tail section. Although Macquarie perch grow to more than 50 cm and 3.5 kg in weight, specimens of this size are extremely rare. Most taken are in the order of 500 g to 1.5 kg.

The Macquarie perch is bluish-grey on top, fading to a creamy colour underneath. Its large white iris has also given rise in some areas to the previously mentioned names of white-eye or silver-eye perch.

Large Populations in Dams

The distribution of the Macquarie perch is similar to that of an even rarer native fish: the little known trout cod. The native range of the Macquarie perch is largely limited to the upper reaches of the Murray, Murrumbidgee and Lachlan Rivers — with the heaviest concentrations found in the

The deep cold waters of southern dams are now the most common habitat for Macquarie perch.

Dartmouth, Eildon, Burrinjuck and Wyangala reservoirs located on those rivers — and a few coastal streams.

Fish have also acclimatised in the Yarra and Barwon Rivers in Victoria.

In New South Wales, catches are still recorded in Googong, Burrinjuck, Wyangala and Tallowa Dams, and the rivers above them, but not in any great numbers.

Macquarie perch can also be found in a couple of the major coastal river systems south of Sydney. They were introduced into Warragamba Dam, west of Sydney, but fishing there is prohibited. Scientists monitoring Sydney's water supply sometimes use the Macquarie perch to gauge the levels of pollution and presence of possible toxic substances in the city's drinking water.

A good supply of fish has been found in the Nepean River and catches have been made as far downstream as the Colo River junction, at Lower Portland.

Light Tackle Appropriate

A whippy 2 m rod and 3 kg line is a good choice of tackle combined with a single split shot, a short leader around 90 cm and a No. 4 hook.

Macquarie perch have the frustrating habit of either playing with the bait or ignoring it. When this happens, it could be worthwhile changing to a smaller No. 8 or 10 hook. It's also a good idea to let the fish run a few metres with the hook before attempting to set it.

Natural Baits are Best

Macquarie perch are primarily captured on natural baits. Their diet includes shrimps, yabbies, small fish, worms, insects and insect larvae. When they are feeding on the surface, a floating line and a greased leader have a lot of potential.

Many captures have been made by anglers fishing for trout with dry flies; others have fallen to wet flies and streamer patterns. One of the best techniques is to drift a nymph, such as a mudeye or stonefly imitation, in a likely-looking pool.

Sometimes these fish will fall to a wobbler or spinner, but on many occasions they will only follow a lure with great curiosity and refuse to strike.

Feeding Grounds

Macquarie perch tend to congregate near weed beds, close to underwater timber, and alongside the main current in the stream. Sandbanks are a favoured spot, particularly where the water swirls around a sloping sandbank to form eddies.

In these sandy-bottomed or sandy bankside spots, worms and shrimps are extremely effective baits.

Flighty Customers

In the same manner as trout, Macquarie perch can be very wary of man's presence in bankside fishing spots. Any heavy tramping of feet, undue noise, or shadows cast across the water will put the fish off. If an angler is quiet and unobtrusive, the fish can be enticed to feed practically at the water's edge.

The best feeding times appear to be the early evening, although fish have been taken at any time during the day. They are also known to come on the bite at the onset of a thunderstorm, when distant, rumbling thunder can be heard. They tend to steer clear of direct sunlight and prefer patches of water near shade.

Diminishing Stocks

For many years now, the Macquarie perch has failed to re-establish itself in many parts of its range, with the result that stocks are diminishing. Spawning occurs during spring/summer in shallow, fast-flowing water over gravel beds, and the resultant eggs adhere to the gravel.

These spawning grounds in many inland rivers have been eroded, destroyed or altered by either man or nature. The construction of dams and weirs, deforestation and siltation have all contributed to the destruction of the fish's natural environment and fishing pressure has been exerted on the survivors. There is also another factor which influences survival: although female fish are extremely fertile, males require two years to reach maturity and females three years.

Macquarie perch may not be plentiful, but taking the odd fish now and then should not present problems. However, in areas where they are extremely scarce, releasing the fish would be the most sensible practice. Many anglers today, concerned over the future of the Macquarie perch, are reluctant to kill one they have hooked up. Although the eating quality of this fish is extremely good, with white, fine-textured flesh, there are other more abundant freshwater fish for those in search of a fish meal.

AUSTRALIAN BASS

The Australian bass is surrounded by mystique and legend, based largely on its ability to strike lures and flies with a ferocity out of all proportion to its size. While the fight is usually only short-lived, it is often intense and dramatic if the fish burrows its way into snags or weed beds.

Ideal bass water can be large or small rivers, creeks, swamps or marshes, but the fish usually prefers relatively deep and clean water, with a moderate flow and good bankside shade. It should also have clear downstream access to salt water — such as an estuary — so the bass can travel there each autumn or winter to spawn, and the area must support a wide variety of prey, including crustaceans, small fish and aquatic and waterside insect life on which the bass can feed.

That qualifies most of the coastal strip of country from southern Queensland right through New South Wales to northern Victoria as potential bass water. This comprises the modern-day range of the bass, though it is extended in the south and west by the range of the very closely related estuary perch, which is found from northern New South Wales to western Victoria and northern Tasmania.

A Fly in the Ointment

Bass inhabit the same area as the majority of Australia's population, which has meant major impacts on its habitat. Bass need streams that have a saltwater estuary attached so they can breed.

Land clearing, siltation, pollution and dams and weirs have all combined to have a negative effect on bass numbers. However, there are still plenty of bass around, particularly in the few undammed rivers left in coastal areas.

Even the Nepean River with all its environmental problems still has plenty of bass available upstream from Wisemans Ferry.

Better Bass Fishing

The best way to conserve bass stocks and still fish for them is to practise catch and release for the bulk of your catch, only keeping enough fish for your immediate needs. Go ahead, catch all you like, but only kill what you really need to, and there'll be more and better fish for a long time to come.

Territorial Creatures

Bass can be found anywhere in a coastal stream from the brackish zone at the tidal limit right up into the mountain streams and pools. Only high waterfalls and dams will prevent their distribution.

The fish is extremely territorial and sets up camp where it has both cover and access to passing food. Bass particularly like snags, undercut banks, heavy bankside cover that droops into the water, sheer rocky walls and the edges of weed beds.

From this feeding station, bass will burst out and devour almost anything that passes by which they think will fit in their mouth.

Lures Ideal

Bass are a prime candidate for capture on lures because of their aggressive nature.

In the deep, slow-flowing stretches of rivers small strong-actioned plugs work well. Both shallow-running and deep-diving lures can be used depending on the time of day.

In the early morning or late afternoon the bass are likely to be close to the surface of the water and shallow divers work well. Once the sun is high in the sky deep divers work best.

When fishing to snags and likely spots the lures are often cast and allowed a few seconds to settle. The lure is then twitched a few times with little flicks of the rod tip.

The twitching simulates insects which may have fallen into the water and often results in a crashing strike. If no strike is forthcoming, then a slow, jerky retrieve is used.

Further upstream where bass inhabit the running water and pools, medium-sized bladed lures and small strong-actioned plugs work best.

Surface Lures

At dusk and into the evening, surface lures like Jitterbugs and Crazy Crawlers will draw strikes from bass. Cast them close to any solid timber or rock, as these often draw fish like a magnet.

You'll get more fish by letting the lure sit motionless for a few seconds. Then start a slow, irregular retrieve, with twitches and pauses rather than winding the lure straight in.

Flies can be effective on bass, too, especially the fuzzy, big-bodied kind. Fish these as floaters, much as you would a surface popper, with short sharp tugs to make them 'bloop' and send out small shock waves like a frog or grasshopper swimming.

Casting to snags from small dinghies or canoes is a popular and productive way of catching bass.

The Bass Season and Bass Baits

While you can catch them in the spring and autumn, bass are generally best fished for during summer, when the hot, steamy evenings and cool, clear mornings promote plenty of insect movement and provide the bass with a good supply of active food items.

In late spring in most freshwater rivers, there is an explosion in the local shrimp population. These can be scooped from weed beds with a fine-mesh scoop or gathered in traps baited with meat.

Fish big shrimps on tiny fine-wire hooks passed once through the tail, or if the shrimps are really tiny, stick a few at a time onto the hook to make a more substantial bait.

Other than shrimps, baits can be a variety of naturally occurring food items, like crickets, grasshoppers, cicadas, gudgeons or worms.

Fish the insects as surface baits and the worms and gudgeons near the bottom under a float with a tiny split shot to keep the bait deep.

Dirty Fighters

When hooked the bass's first instinct is to dive back to the protective cover of its hiding place. Large bass can be a real handful on sporting tackle and anglers need quick reflexes to turn them away from cover.

If a hooked bass does snag you, release the pressure immediately and wait to see if the fish will swim out. They often do.

Bass are good fighters but they tire quickly once coaxed away from their snaggy lair. Just be prepared for that explosive strike.

Eating Qualities

Bass are good eating, tasting very much like silver bream. It is always best to take the smaller fish for the table rather than the big breeders needed to regenerate the stock.

A happy angler with a small bass.

CATFISH

Often disregarded by anglers due to their appearance, both the saltwater and freshwater catfish are good eating and represent worthwhile light-tackle fishing for many anglers in some of the more remote parts of the country.

There are well over 1000 species of catfish in the world, most of which live in fresh water. All species are characterised by thick, scaleless skin and the 'cat's whiskers': long feelers or barbels which encircle the mouth and give the fish its cat-like appearance. Australian catfish may be roughly classified into eel-tailed or blunt-tailed catfish and the fork-tailed species.

Catfish come in a variety of sizes. The giant salmon catfish grows to as much as 27 kg, whereas the tiny Berney's catfish, common in the many streams that flow into the Gulf of Carpentaria, rarely exceeds 25 cm.

Mouth Brooders

Some species of catfish have interesting mating characteristics. The males use their fins to scoop a hollow in the river bed and then build a nest of pebbles; with eel-tailed catfish, this nest generally measures up to 1 m in width and up to 70 cm in height.

After the female lays her eggs in the nest, they are guarded by the male until they hatch. In some species, the male actually carries the eggs in his mouth until they hatch, and after that, the young fish still retreat back into their father's mouth when danger threatens. The males do not eat while they are 'mouth-brooding' the eggs.

Eel-tailed Catfish

The eel-tailed catfish is one of the most common native freshwater fish of coastal streams and rivers, inland waterways, dams and reservoirs. It provides first-rate fishing for inland anglers and is an excellent table fish.

This fish is sometimes sold under the name of jewfish, dewfish and butterfish, and shouldn't be confused with the marine jewfish or mulloway. Like other catfish, the eel-tailed catfish has tough and slimy scaleless skin and an eel-type fin that extends the entire length of the body.

The body is a mottled dark olive green to very light beige, depending on whether the specimen is taken from clear or muddy waters. It grows to a length of about 1 m and a weight of 6 kg.

The most commonly known eel-tailed catfish (*Tandanus tandanus*) is found in the Murray–Darling river system and in adjacent lagoons and swamps, extending into some of the larger east coast rivers. The Clarence and Nepean Rivers in New South Wales carry good stocks in their upper reaches and the fish also inhabit the river systems of Queensland.

Bottom Feeders

The eel-tailed catfish feeds mostly on the bottom of rivers. It spends a great deal of time foraging and scavenging through the organic debris that has already been sifted by fish higher in the pecking order.

It feeds on mussels, shrimps, yabbies and worms. Any of these make good baits. Also favoured are peeled crayfish tails, earthworms and wood grubs. However, the freshwater mussel seems to be the most effective bait with a standard river rod, a 3.5 kg line and a No. 2 hook.

Usually eel-tailed catfish will not accept a lure, but they have been hooked after mistaking the lure for an 'intruder' that has come too close to their nest. The eel-tailed catfish is one of our few native fish that breed well and grow satisfactorily in small water impoundments and weirs.

Good Sport on Light Tackle

The eel-tailed catfish puts up a good fight on light gear. Its usual tactic is to head for snags and weeds from which it can be difficult for the angler to dislodge it. Unweighted baits and light lines will bring more bites than the heavier traditional type of set line, although the latter is frequently used by inland anglers.

Where sinkers are necessary, the standard inland bottom rig with a running sinker and a swivel tied 30 cm above the hook is very effective. For fishing in reedy, swampy areas, a small quill float should be used to keep the bait above the weeds.

Handle with Care

The eel-tailed catfish's sharp spines along the leading edges of the dorsal and pectoral

Catfish are good eating.

fins are regarded as venomous and should be handled with care. They can cause considerable tissue damage and severe pain to careless hands.

Superb Table Fish

Among inland anglers, the eel-tailed catfish rates very highly as a table fish. Its white, moist flesh is well flavoured and the fish is easily prepared by skinning and filleting. Many country folk prefer the catfish to the golden perch or yellowbelly and when served cold, the flesh has an appeal not unlike that of some of the large crustaceans.

For years, these mouth-watering fish were thrown away or used as bait to catch 'better' fish. It took two generations of migrants to convince the local fishing fraternity that they were discarding superb table fish.

Fork-tailed Catfish

Catfish are also captured by anglers in the north of Western Australia. This species has a forked tail and three poisonous spines. These fish travel far into the freshwater rivers and inland pools, and will accept almost any kind of flesh bait. Although the northern catfish does not have the same delicious flavour as the southern species, many relish its thick steaks which can be filleted and grilled to make a good meal.

REDFIN

One of the most prolific fish in our inland rivers, lakes and reservoirs, the redfin – also known as English perch – is an ideal fish for beginners and experienced anglers alike. It can be taken on warm sunny days using a wide variety of baits and lures, and it is prevalent in many inland waterways.

With its gaping mouth, insatiable appetite and willingness to take almost any bait presented, the redfin has been called 'almost suicidal' in its attempts to become hooked.

However, this description mainly applies to small and medium-sized fish. As the fish get to their larger sizes they stop schooling and become solitary, canny customers, hiding in sheltered positions along riverbanks and under submerged logs.

Introduced Species

The redfin was introduced from England by well-meaning colonists into the rivers of Tasmania in 1862, and later into the waterways of other states. Many anglers regret that such an event occurred at all.

Redfin relish young trout and trout eggs, and are in direct competition for food with the Murray cod, golden perch and other native fish. However, small redfin are eaten by golden perch and Murray cod, so nature seems to have struck a balance.

The redfin and golden perch coexist quite well in some waters. The native perch has an overall advantage, as it can tolerate warmer waters and is hardier than the redfin.

Wide-ranging Distribution

The redfin is found in great numbers in the Murray–Darling river system and in the many lakes and reservoirs in Victoria. It is particularly abundant in Eildon Lake in Victoria and also in Tasmanian waters. In South Australia, rivers like the Torrens, Light, Finniss, North and South Para all contain good stocks of redfin.

The fish flourishes in many New South Wales rivers, particularly in the central and southern regions. In Western Australia, redfin are found in the south-west region where they are concentrated in the Blackwood River and its tributaries.

The higher temperatures of far-western and northern streams have checked the spread of redfin in these directions. Experts have found that the fish cannot tolerate water temperatures over 31°C.

Humpbacked Appearance

Redfin have a dark, humped back which fades to a yellowish, brassy colour on the flanks, with five to six bands of olive green running across the body. The belly fins and lower tail are usually bright orange-red, while the pectoral fin is sharply spined and can cause a few handling problems for anglers without a landing net.

Redfin have the ability to blend with their environment, so colour variations do occur. Those captured in Lake Eildon, Victoria, tend to be more silvery in colour than those taken from the Murray River. When the fish is threatened, it pales quickly and this can help it blend with its immediate surroundings.

Stocks of Stunted Fish

The redfin spawns in late winter or early spring, among aquatic plants and away from fast currents. The redfin is exceptionally prolific, with one mature fish capable of producing more than 100,000 ova.

Because of this fecundity, fish around 10 cm are able to breed and this results in populations of very stunted fish in many streams. For example, in the lower Lachlan River and Blowering Dam in New South Wales, the redfin are so small that fishing is hardly worthwhile.

Quiet Habitat

The redfin does not favour fast-flowing waters. It tends to shelter under submerged logs and in the vicinity of weed beds, preferring the still waters of quiet back-reaches of rivers. It will only swim against currents when rivers are flooded.

The redfin also prefers cool to cold waters, which is why it thrives in Victoria and Tasmania. Schools often lie close to the bottom, around drowned trees, overhanging vegetation or similar weedy cover. Another popular hiding spot is under the undercut banks of rivers, particularly where these are sheltered by tussocks or weeds.

Bait and Tackle

The redfin's diet includes yabbies, shrimps, mudeyes and worms. The redfin will also accept baits of small fish such as carp, Galaxiids or minnows and the small *Gambusia* or mosquito fish (which is usually hooked carefully through the lower jaw to keep it alive).

Red, wriggling worms are a top bait with garden worms next best. Many anglers have great success by hooking worms just once through the middle, rather than threading them on the hook.

No specialist tackle is required to catch redfin. A light rod of about 2 m long, a 3 kg line and a No. 4 to No. 1 hook are the basic equipment necessary. Even handlines can be used to take redfin.

Hook sizes will vary depending upon the size of the fish you're chasing and the size of the bait. Although the record catch for a redfin stands at just over 10 kg, very few fish around 5 kg are taken and most fish landed are between 500 g and 1 kg.

Lures and Flies

There are a number of freshwater lures that will arouse redfin. Small, deep-diving plugs, medium-sized bladed spinners and metal spoons are all effective fish-takers. Shiny leadfish-type lures can be dropped to the bottom and bounced a short distance in each direction. Known as bobbing or jigging, this practice results in some huge captures.

Both trolling and spinning will get results, with trolling a good option for locating a school of fish and then spinning or bobbing can be used to catch more of the excited school.

In some of the larger lakes, good catches have been made with wet flies. A streamer or Matuka pattern, cast with spinning tackle and a few split shot for casting weight, can be great sport. The fish can also be taken using regulation fly tackle.

Wait Before Striking

When fishing with baits around snags, a bubble or quill float in the rig can help avoid being constantly tangled in the timber. Fished a foot or so above the river bed, the bait is more likely to arouse the fish's curiosity.

When your worm bait hits the water, flip over the bail arm of the reel and hold the rod out over the water, more or less pointing to where you have cast.

The worms will sink to the bottom, twisting and wriggling and enticing any hungry redfin to the area. When your bait has hit bottom, draw about half a metre of line in and at the same time, lift your rod tip slightly. Drop the tip again and wind in the line you have just created.

Let the worms sink to the bottom again and repeat the action with the rod and line. This 'sink and draw' technique can be very successful with redfin. In a feeding mood, the fish will swim close to your bait and suck it in. You should wait until the fish swims away, then strike.

As with most inland fishing, always move quietly, keeping well back from the water's edge so that the fish cannot see you. Green or khaki clothing will also help to camouflage your activities. You should steer clear of white or colourful clothes.

Preparation for Cooking

The sweet, white flesh of the redfin is good eating. However, it is much drier than that of most other inland fish. Preparing it for the table takes a bit more effort.

Even the best fish scalers are useless on the tough hide of this fish: filleting is the best solution. The fillet can then be skinned with a sharp knife from the tail end, holding the skin firmly with a pair of pliers. A recipe that tends to keep the flesh moist and well flavoured is the best way to prepare redfin.

A strongly marked redfin from Lake Burrinjuck.

EUROPEAN CARP

Introduced into this country more than 100 years ago, the European carp is now so abundant in many freshwater streams that it effectively competes with our native fish. Although regarded as a pest by many inland anglers, carp provide good sport for anglers.

Large, Heavy Scales

The body shape of the carp ranges from streamlined and slender to humped-back and large. The fish has a single dorsal fin, a stout spine and a forked tail.

The carp is characterised by large, heavy scales, a small rubber-lipped mouth and two pairs of barbels or 'whiskers'. Species variations include the scaleless leather carp and the odd-looking mirror carp with its few, widely spaced scales.

The carp's body colour differs from species to species, but is mostly olive green to gold on the back, brassy yellow on the sides and creamy yellow below. Variations can range from milky white through piebald to bright orange. Fins are dusky, often with a red tinge.

Prefers Warm BackWaters

Slow-moving pools, billabongs and warm rivers are the preferred habitat of carp. They particularly like streams with muddy bottoms.

Carp feed by sucking up mud and plants, ejecting them and selecting material floating in the water. The warmer the water, the more the carp will bite. Their diet includes weeds, insect larvae, worms, snails and other small creatures.

Because of their feeding action or roiling, carp stir up mud on the bottom, leaving dark clouds of silt in the water.

It is this roiling action which makes the carp despised by some anglers. Roiling often leaves a freshwater stream muddy and unfit for other fish which rely on sight to locate their food.

It can also limit the amount of sunlight necessary for aquatic plant growth, and it may cause silt from the bottom to settle on the spawn of other fish. Carp may also suck in the eggs and fry of other fish and it is all these habits which cause the ecologist and inland angler to look with disdain on the carp.

Spawning

In the winter months, carp hibernate, gathering in schools in deeper parts of lakes and streams. They then move into shallow water to spawn, with the female laying more than 1,000,000 eggs. In tropical waters, the eggs may hatch within 36 hours. Carp are predators and both parents and young fish are possible victims of carp larger than themselves.

INLAND SPORT FISH

In spite of varied opinions, carp have been a boon to freshwater anglers as they are relatively easy to catch and readily available.

Any backwater which is open to a main river in New South Wales, South Australia, Victoria and Tasmania will usually produce carp and so will some that have been closed off.

In shallow swamps, individual fish can be seen swimming along with their backs out of water. They also seem to like lying half-submerged on shallow banks, basking in the sun.

BASIC TACKLE IS BEST

When fishing backwaters and slow-moving streams for carp, almost any combination of rod, reel, hook and sinker will catch these fish. However, a 3 m rod with a very light and sensitive tip, combined with a small threadline reel and a 4 kg breaking strain line, is recommended.

Fish up to 9 kg can be expected in some streams and any size fish can be landed with this gear if the drag is set so that the fish can take the line. Carp have very soft mouths and if heavier gear is used, the hook will pull out when too much pressure is applied.

The best hooks are bronzed bait holders from size No. 6 up to 2/0. Sinker sizes depend on weather conditions and on how far it's necessary to cast to reach the fish. The stronger the wind, the heavier the sinker should be, so it pays to carry a range of ball sinkers up to 28 g. A heavier sinker

A carp caught in the Nepean River near Sydney.

in windy conditions will prevent a large bow forming in the line.

There are three rigs in general use. The first has a sinker tied to the end of the line with the hook on a 15 cm trace above the sinker. The second is a conventional bream rig which consists of a small ball sinker running freely on the main line above a 45 cm trace. Only one hook should be used if trying to land a big fish as a second hook could become snagged.

Fishing with a small float suspending the bait off the bottom is also an extremely popular method of hooking carp.

MOST BAITS ACCEPTABLE

Popular baits used to catch carp in Australia are very much the same as those used in Europe. Carp are not fussy eaters and will accept worms, maggots, shrimps, mussels, yabby tails, bread, cheese and wood grubs. They can also be caught with corn, dough and meat.

However, the best bait is undoubtedly any kind of worm, particularly scrub worms or hill worms. They grow up to 30 cm long, are as thick as a man's finger and can be found in loamy soil along the banks of inland streams. They are a very tough worm and it's possible to catch about a dozen large fish on one bait, using about 4 cm of worm threaded onto the hook.

Carp will also fall to smallish, soft baits such as 'pudding' mixtures, dough, parboiled potatoes and sweet corn niblets. Floating bread crusts and float-suspended maggots are also effective, particularly when used with berley.

Carp will take a fly or small lure on occasions. Although these fish can be ridiculously easy to tempt, large carp in still water can still be extremely wary, so the angler needs to use good bait, rig correctly and be careful with the approach: in this case, use light tackle and a stealthy approach.

Technique

When casting into a shallow backwater, the sinker will often stick in the mud. Always pull the sinker forward a couple of feet before placing the rod on a rod rest to wait for a bite. Let the fish play with the bait for a while and only strike when it applies a steady pressure on the rod tip.

Anglers should play the fish until it is exhausted. By then the angler will be able to put his or her fingers in the gills and lift it out of the water.

Eating Qualities

Carp is considered a delicacy in some European countries and is associated with holiday feasts. In Australia, many people of European and Asian descent still have a preference for the fish. However, for the majority of Australians raised on other types of fish, the carp is not too highly regarded as a table fish because of its coarse flesh, many bones and muddy taste.

A carp this size will put up a great struggle on light tackle.

INDEX